Map Skills for Today

Grade 2

Take a Trip With Us

Map Skills for Today
Take a Trip With Us
Grade 2

Publisher: Keith Garton
Editorial Director: Maureen Hunter-Bone
Editorial Development: Summer Street Press, LLC
Writer: Susan Buckley
Project Editor: Miriam Aronin
Editor: Alex Giannini
Design and Production: Dinardo Design, LLC
Photo Editor: Kim Babbitt

Illustration Credits: Stephanie Powers
Map Credits: Mapping Specialists, Ltd.
Photo Credits: Page 4: SuperStock, John Klein/Weekly Reader; Page 8: Alan Schein Photography/Corbis, David Jay Zimmerman/Corbis; Page 10: Joson/zefa/Corbis, George Hall/Corbis, Jupiter Images; Page 11: Jupiter Images; Page 35: Geostock/Getty Images; Page 41: Jupiter Images, IndexOpen, Jochen Schlenker/Masterfile, Photodisc/Getty, Jupiter Images, Photodisc/Getty

Teachers: Go online to www.scholastic.com/mapskillsfortoday for teaching ideas and the answer key.

ISBN: 978-1-338-21489-5

1 2 3 4 5 6 7 8 9 10   40   23 22 21 20 19 18

Take a Trip With Us

Table of Contents

What Is a Globe?

Hi,

We are Jordan and Jamie, two friends who like to travel to different places. Come on a trip with us! We're going to study and learn about maps from the Mapmaker. We'll travel to different places to find out more about our world.

Yours truly,

Jordan and Jamie

Dear Jamie and Jordan,

Let's start our trip. We're going to find out more about our planet, Earth. Look at this photograph of Earth. Some people call Earth "a big blue marble"!

What if you want to find a place on Earth? You can use a globe. A **globe** is a small model of Earth. Like that "big blue marble," a globe is round. Like a marble or a ball, a globe is a sphere. You can turn it around so you can see all the different parts of Earth.

Yours truly,

Mapmaker

Think It Over

1. How are a globe and a photograph of Earth the same?

2. How are they different?

Earth's Land and Water

Look at the photograph of Earth on page 4. You can see land and water on Earth. The large areas of land are **continents**. The large areas of water are **oceans**.

Now look at this picture of a globe. You can see two continents on this globe. They are North America and South America. We live in North America.

You can see four oceans on this globe. They are the Atlantic Ocean, the Pacific Ocean, the Southern Ocean, and the Arctic Ocean.

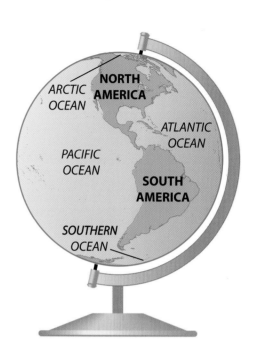

Use Your Skills

Circle the words to finish each sentence.

1. A globe is _____ .

   flat   round

2. A globe is a _____ of Earth.

   model   part

3. Continents are large areas of

   _____ .

   land   water

4. Oceans are large areas of

   _____ .

   land   water

5. We live on the continent of

   _____ America.

   North   South

6. The _____ Ocean is a large area of water.

   North   Atlantic

Your Turn Now

Let's take an imaginary trip! Find a globe. Close your eyes, spin the globe around, and put your finger on a place. Where did you land? Would you like to go there? Why or why not?

What Is a Map?

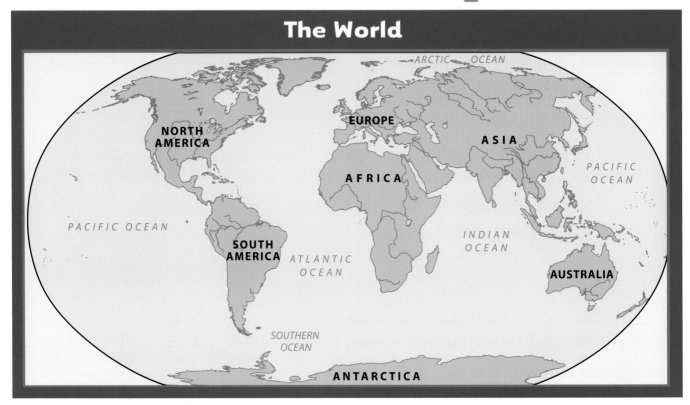

The World

NORTH AMERICA

EUROPE

ASIA

AFRICA

SOUTH AMERICA

AUSTRALIA

ANTARCTICA

ARCTIC OCEAN

PACIFIC OCEAN

PACIFIC OCEAN

ATLANTIC OCEAN

INDIAN OCEAN

SOUTHERN OCEAN

A **map** is a special kind of drawing of a place. A globe is round, but a map is flat, like a piece of paper.

Some maps, like globes, show the whole Earth at once. The map on this page shows the seven continents of the world. It shows oceans, too.

 Think It Over

1. How easy would it be to carry a globe around? How could a map be simpler to use?

2. How are a globe and a map the same?

3. How are they different?

4. Which is better for seeing more at once, a world map or a globe?

What Maps Show

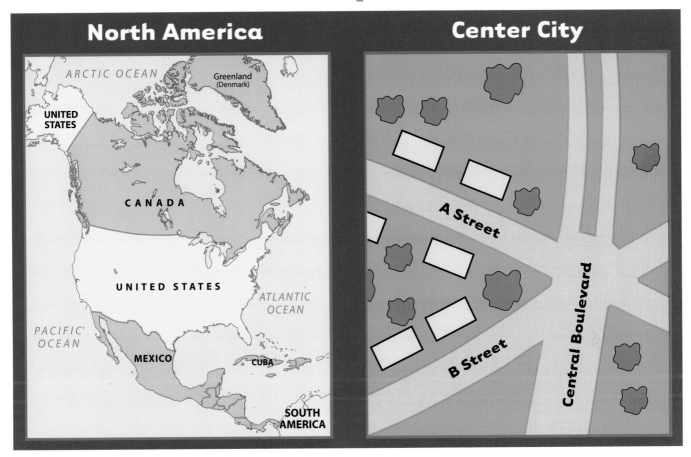

North America

ARCTIC OCEAN

Greenland (Denmark)

UNITED STATES

CANADA

UNITED STATES

ATLANTIC OCEAN

PACIFIC OCEAN

MEXICO

CUBA

SOUTH AMERICA

Center City

A Street

B Street

Central Boulevard

Some maps show a large part of Earth. Other maps show a smaller area.

Use Your Skills

The maps on pages 6 and 7 will help you answer these questions.

1. Write a **W** on the world map.

2. Find all seven continents on the world map. They are shown in green. Number them from **1** to **7**.

3. Find our continent, North America, on the world map. Circle it.

4. Now look at the map of North America on this page. Find the United States on this map. Draw a ★ on it.

5. Look at the map of Center City. You want to meet a friend where A Street meets Central Boulevard. Put a ✔ at that spot on the map.

Your Turn Now

Think of someplace you would like to go. Find a map that would help you get there.

A View from Above

A map is a special view of Earth. It is a view from above.

If you were walking down the street, you might see a view like this.

If you were in an airplane, you might see a view like this.

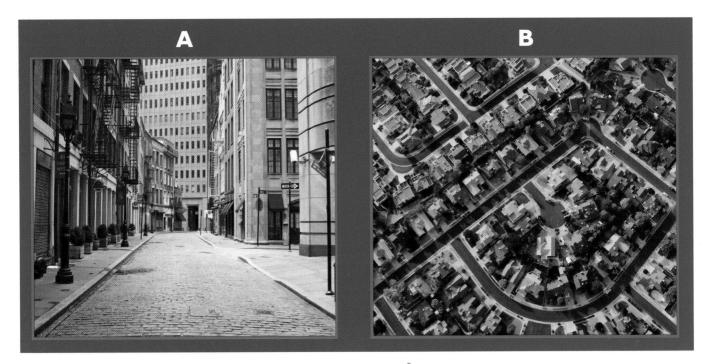

A

B

Pretend that you are a mapmaker. You could draw a map that looks like picture B. Both are views from above.

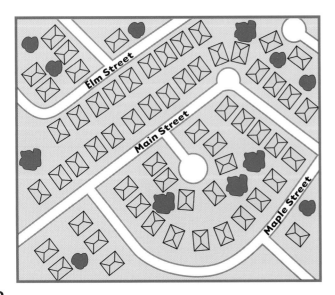

Use Your Skills

1. Find a house in picture B and on the map. Write a ✓ on each.

2. Find a road in picture B and on the map. Write an ✗ on each.

Think It Over

What are some differences between picture B and the map? How would these make the map useful?

All Around the Park

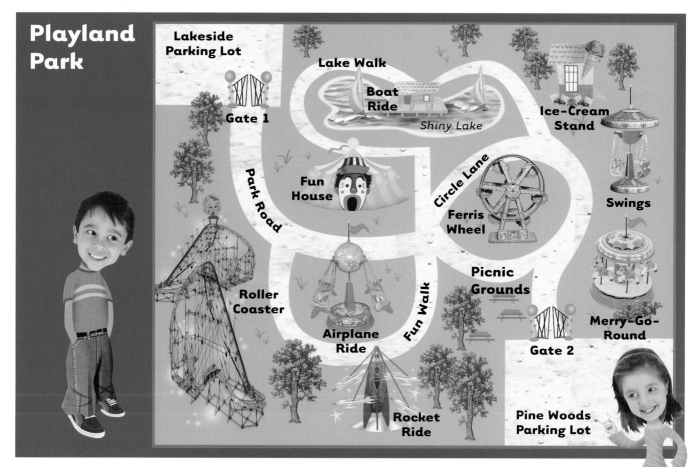

Playland Park

Lakeside Parking Lot · Gate 1 · Lake Walk · Boat Ride · Shiny Lake · Ice-Cream Stand · Swings · Park Road · Fun House · Circle Lane · Ferris Wheel · Roller Coaster · Picnic Grounds · Fun Walk · Airplane Ride · Gate 2 · Merry-Go-Round · Rocket Ride · Pine Woods Parking Lot

Jamie and Jordan are visiting Playland Park. The park is large. They use a map to find their way around. The map is a view of the park from above.

⭐ Use Your Skills

Jamie and Jordan must decide where to enter the park. These are the places they want to see:

Merry-Go-Round   Ferris Wheel

Swings   Fun House

1. Circle each place on the map.

Jamie and Jordan want to go to the Merry-Go-Round first.

2. Find Gate 1 and Gate 2. Which gate should Jamie and Jordan use? Write a ✓ by that gate.

3. Draw a line on the road to show how Jamie and Jordan might walk through the park.

What Are Map Symbols?

Mapmakers use symbols to show things on a map. A symbol stands for something that is real. Some symbols are pictures like these. They look like what they stand for.

Use Your Skills

1. One of the symbols above stands for a house. Write HOUSE next to the correct symbol.

2. What does the other symbol stand for? Write the word next to the symbol.

3. Match these symbols with the photographs.

Your Turn Now

Suppose you want to draw a map of your room. Draw your own symbols here.

Table

Bed

Chair

TV

Special Map Symbols

Mapmakers use lines, shapes, and colors as symbols. Photo A shows a road. So does Map A. The map uses a symbol to show the road. Look at Photo B. What symbol on Map B shows the bridge?

 **Your Turn Now**

 Use Your Skills

A lake is a body of water with land all around it. Look at this photograph of a lake. Draw a symbol for a lake.

Underline each sentence that is true according to the maps on this page.

1. Both maps show roads.

2. The color blue shows water.

3. Map A shows a river.

4. Both maps show bridges.

5. Land is shown by the color green.

A

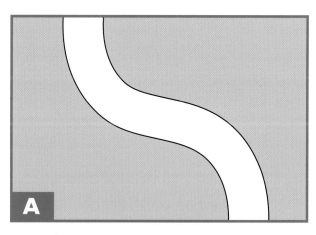

A

B

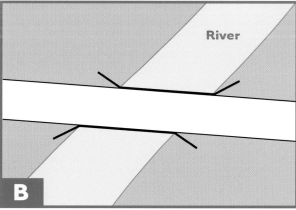

River

B

Using Map Symbols

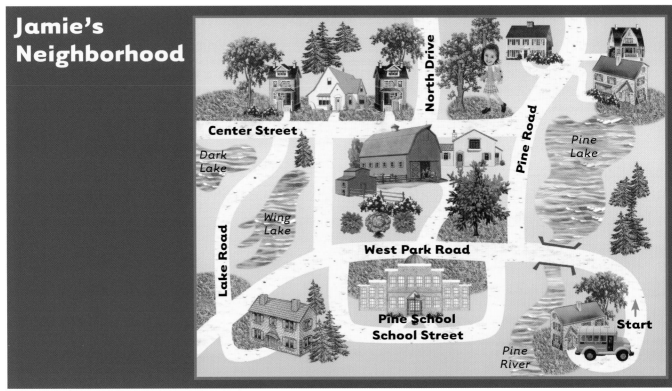

Jamie's Neighborhood

North Drive

Center Street

Dark Lake

Pine Road

Pine Lake

Lake Road

Wing Lake

West Park Road

Pine School
School Street

Pine River

Start

The map above shows Jamie's neighborhood. It is what mapmakers call a picture map. The pictures on the map show different buildings and places. You can trace Jamie's route to school on this picture map. The pictures will help you.

Use Your Skills

1. Jamie rides to school on a bus. Find the bus on the map. Draw a ★ where the bus starts.

2. Begin tracing Jamie's trip. The bus crosses the bridge and turns right.

3. The bus turns left at the next corner. It stops to pick up Jamie. What is Jamie standing next to?

_____

4. The bus goes to the blue house and turns left. What two lakes does it pass? _____

_____

5. The last stop is at the school. What is the name of the school?

_____

Jamie's Neighborhood

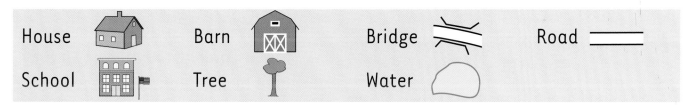

Most mapmakers use symbols instead of pictures. These are the symbols that were used to make this map of Jamie's neighborhood. You can use the symbols and labels on the map to trace Jamie's trip home from school.

House		Barn		Bridge		Road
School		Tree		Water		

 **Map It!**

Follow these directions. Draw a line on the map to trace the trip.

1. Jamie's school is on School Street. Write START in front of the school.

2. The bus goes to West Park Road and turns left. Then it turns right on Lake Road. Write a **1** on the first lake the bus passes.

3. Then the bus turns right on Center Street. After the bus passes the corner of Center Street and North Drive, it stops by the tree. Mark a **J** where Jamie gets out.

 **Think It Over**

Why do you think mapmakers use symbols?

What Is a Map Key?

Key

School　House　Road　Lake　Bridge

Put a key in a lock, and you can open a door. Maps have keys, too. A **map key** helps you unlock the "door" to a map. It tells you what the symbols on the map stand for.

 Map It!

You can make a map key for a map of Summerville. At the top of page 15 there is a picture map of Summerville. Jordan is going there for a vacation.

Use Map A for these activities.

1. Find Jordan on Map A. Put a ★ next to his picture.

2. Circle the Best Hotel. That is where Jordan is staying.

3. Trace a route from the Best Hotel to Summerville Beach. That is the beach where Jordan will swim. Put an **S** on the beach.

Jordan has learned how to use a map with symbols and a key. He wants to take one on his trip. Complete Map B for Jordan.

4. Look at the symbols on Map B. Find the symbol that looks like this ▭. Circle it. Then look at Map A. Look at the picture in the same position and read the label. What does this symbol stand for? Circle the correct answer.

   beach　hotel　railroad station

5. Find the same symbol in the map key on Map B. Write the correct name next to the symbol.

6. Fill in the names next to each symbol in the map key. Use Map A for clues.

Summerville

Map A

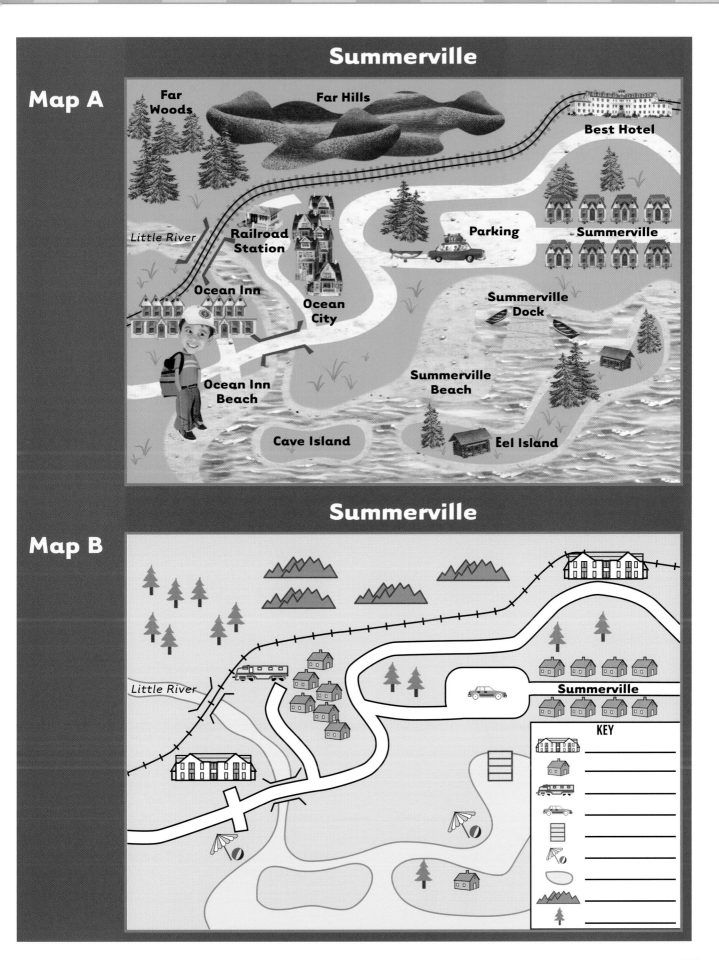

Far Woods

Far Hills

Best Hotel

Little River

Railroad Station

Parking

Summerville

Ocean Inn

Ocean City

Summerville Dock

Ocean Inn Beach

Summerville Beach

Cave Island

Eel Island

Summerville

Map B

Little River

Summerville

KEY

Make a Map
for Jordan and Jamie

You have a chance to make up a place called New City. Then you can give Jordan and Jamie a map so they can find their way around!

 **Map It!**

1. There are lots of houses in New City. Draw a symbol for a house in the map key and label it. Add houses to your map.

2. Draw a symbol for a store in the map key and label it. Add stores to your map.

3. Name the streets in New City. Write the names on the map.

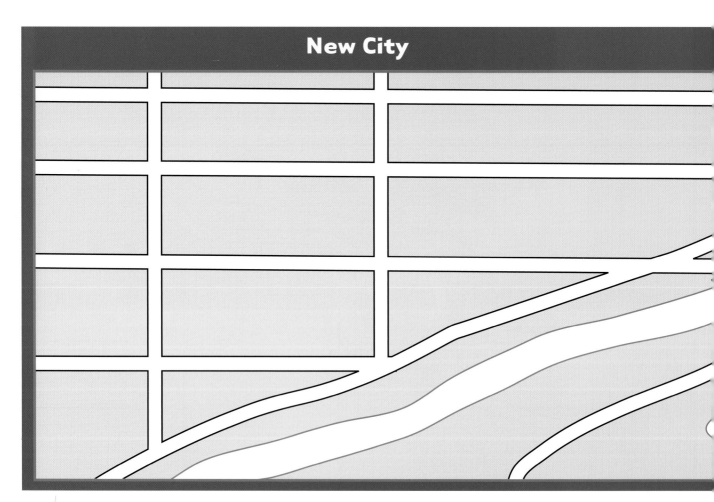

New City

4. There are a river and a lake in New City. Color them blue and name them. Add a blue box to the key and label it WATER.

5. New City has two schools. Draw a symbol for a school in the map key and label it. Add the schools to the map.

6. Find a good place for a park in New City. Draw 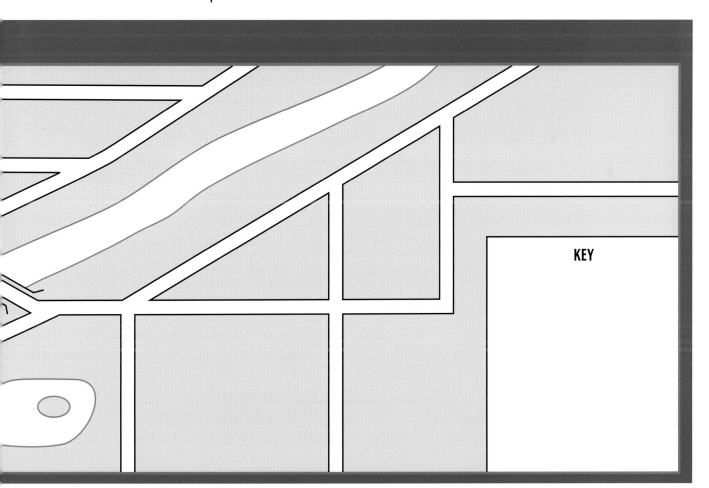 as a symbol for a park in the map key and label it. Show the park on the map. Give it a name and label it on the map.

7. What else would you like to put in New City? Add three more things to the map key and show them on the map.

8. Now plan a nice walk for Jordan and Jamie. Draw the route on the map.

KEY

North, South, East, West

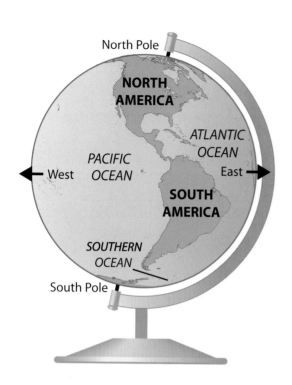

How do you know where you are going and how to get there? **Directions** can help. **North, south, east,** and **west** are directions on Earth.

Look at the globe and find the **North Pole**. Wherever you are on Earth, north is the direction toward the North Pole. Find the **South Pole**. South is the direction toward the South Pole.

When you face north, east is to your right. West is to your left.

 ## Your Turn Now

Find a globe to use for these activities.

1. Touch the North Pole on the globe, then the South Pole.

2. Put your finger on the United States on the globe. Close your eyes and move your finger to the right (east). What ocean is on the east coast of the United States?

3. Do the same thing and move your finger to the left (west). What ocean is on the west coast of the United States?

Up is the direction away from the center of Earth. *Down* is the direction toward the center of Earth.

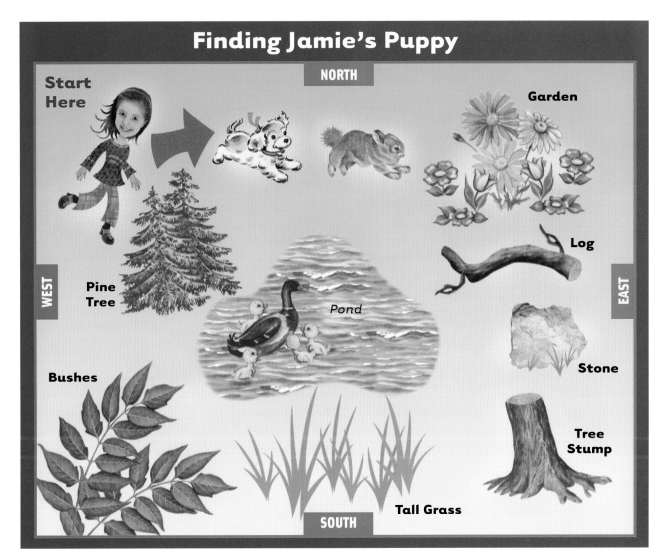

Finding Jamie's Puppy

Start Here

NORTH

Garden

Log

WEST

EAST

Pine Tree

Pond

Stone

Bushes

Tree Stump

Tall Grass

SOUTH

 Use Your Skills

Jamie's puppy chased a rabbit in the park. Draw a line to show which way the puppy and the rabbit went. Use the directions in these sentences to draw your line.

1. The puppy chased the rabbit east into the garden.

2. The rabbit hopped south to the log.

3. The puppy chased the rabbit west to the pine tree.

4. The rabbit ran south to the bushes.

5. The puppy followed the rabbit east to the tall grass.

6. The rabbit hopped north to the pond.

7. The puppy chased the rabbit east to the stone.

8. The rabbit ran south to the tree stump and popped down a hole.

Using Directions

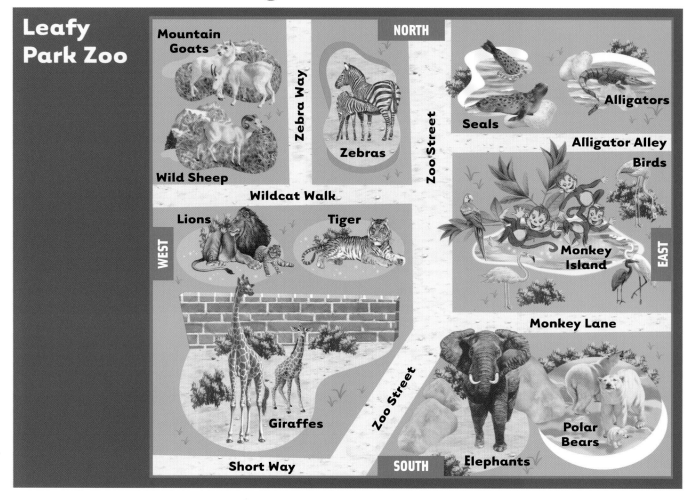

Leafy Park Zoo

NORTH

Mountain Goats

Zebra Way

Zebras

Zoo Street

Seals

Alligators

Alligator Alley

Birds

Wild Sheep

Wildcat Walk

WEST

Lions

Tiger

Monkey Island

EAST

Monkey Lane

Giraffes

Zoo Street

Short Way

SOUTH

Elephants

Polar Bears

Jamie and Jordan are going to visit the zoo. They are using a map to plan their trip. Help them decide where to go.

★ Use Your Skills

Use the picture map to answer these questions. Circle the correct answers.

1. Which of these animals are in the north part of the zoo?

Elephants   Mountain goats

2. Which of these animals are in the south part of the zoo?

Polar bears   Wild sheep

3. Are the lions east or west of the birds?

East   West

4. Are the seals north or south of the monkeys?

North   South

5. Are the alligators east or west of the zebras?

East   West

20

Mapping Directions

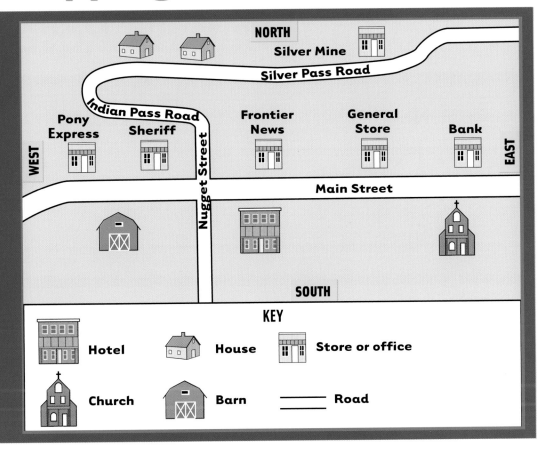

Frontier Town

NORTH
Silver Mine
Silver Pass Road

Indian Pass Road

Pony Express
Sheriff
Frontier News
General Store
Bank

WEST
EAST

Nugget Street

Main Street

SOUTH

KEY
Hotel   House   Store or office
Church   Barn   Road

Use Your Skills

Use the map to plan a trip to Frontier Town.

1. You are going to stay at the Nugget Hotel. Find the hotel on the map and write an **H** on it.

Write the correct direction words on the blanks.

2. When you leave the hotel, your first stop will be the Pony Express office. To get there you will walk _____ on Nugget Street, then _____ on Main Street.

3. After visiting the Pony Express, you want to go to the General Store. You will walk _____ along Main Street.

 Map It!

You can add to the map.

Something is missing on the map. There is a school between the Nugget Hotel and the church. Make up a symbol for a school. Add it to the map and the map key.

What Kind of Rose Is a Compass Rose?

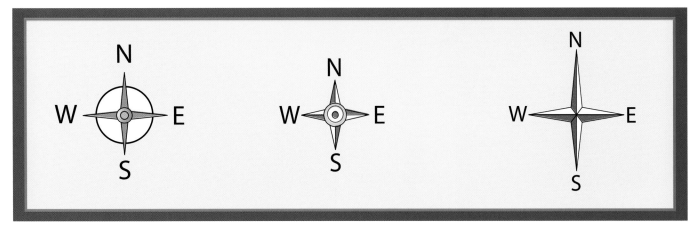

A **compass rose** is a map symbol that shows directions. Look at one compass rose and find north, south, east, and west.

Mapmakers draw different kinds of compass roses. Above are three compass roses. Which do you like best?

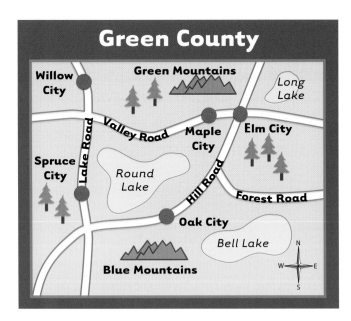

Green County

Your Turn Now

Draw your own compass rose. Tell your classmates about your drawing.

Use Your Skills

Use the picture map to answer these questions.

1. Where is the compass rose on the picture map? Circle it.

2. You drive from Elm City to Maple City. What direction do you drive?

   _____

3. Is Bell Lake north or south of Long Lake? _____

4. Are the Blue Mountains east or west of Bell Lake? _____

5. Are the Blue Mountains north or south of Round Lake? _____

Using a Compass Rose

Pirate Treasure

Black Mountains

Pirate Cave

Crow Island

Forest Road

East Ocean

Treasure Road

Pirate Lake

N
W E
S

Old Oak Tree

Once, Jordan and Jamie found a note and a map about a pirate's buried treasure. The note was in a chest south of Pirate Lake.

- Cross the bridge and go north on Treasure Road to the old house.

- Go north to the Black Mountains.

- Go east to the three trees.

- Use a boat and sail south to the tip of Crow Island.

- Sail to the island closest to the Old Oak Tree.

- Dig under the palm tree.

Map It!

Help Jordan and Jamie find the treasure! Use the compass rose to follow the directions in the note. Mark an **A** at the chest where Jordan and Jamie started. Draw a line to show where they should go. Mark an **X** where they can find treasure.

Your Turn Now

What if Jamie and Jordan found the note in front of Pirate Cave? Start at Pirate Cave and write new directions to the buried treasure.

Visiting New Town

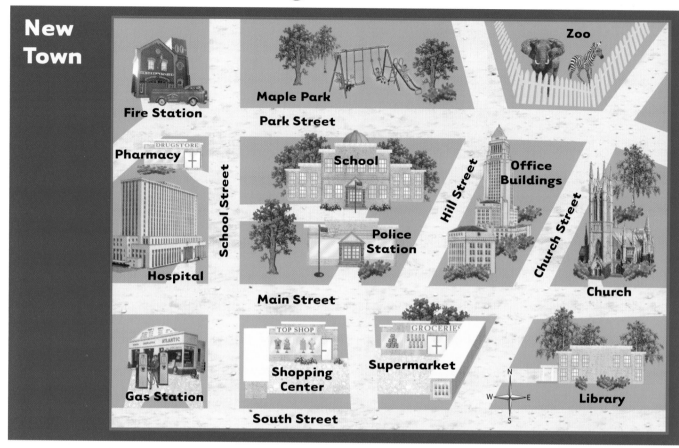

When you study a map to find your way, a compass rose is always useful. Jordan uses the compass rose to learn about New Town. His friend Kelly just moved there.

 **Use Your Skills**

1. Jordan meets Kelly at the library. Find the library on the map and write START next to it.

2. After they leave the library, Kelly and Jordan walk west along South Street. They turn north and walk half a block to the supermarket. Draw their route.

3. Now Jordan and Kelly want to go to Maple Park to eat their lunch. Should they go north or south?

_____

4. Jordan loves to talk to firefighters. Draw a route from the park to the fire station.

5. Time to go home! Jordan's father will pick him up at the library. Draw the shortest route from the fire station to the library.

Jordan's Neighborhood

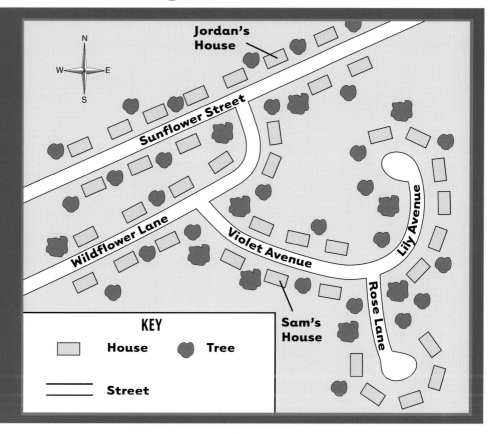

Jordan's Neighborhood

KEY

House   Tree

Street

Families living near one another make up a neighborhood. This is a map of Jordan's neighborhood. Jordan's friend Sam lives in the same neighborhood. You can use the compass rose and key to read the map.

Use Your Skills

1. Fill in the missing directions on the compass rose.

2. Is Sam's house north or south of Jordan's house? _____

3. Does Rose Lane run north-south or east-west? _____

4. Is Violet Avenue north or south of Jordan's house? _____

Map It!

The town is going to build a school in this neighborhood. Where should it go? Add a symbol for to the map and to the map key.

Think It Over

How is this map different from the map of New Town on page 24?

Making Maps

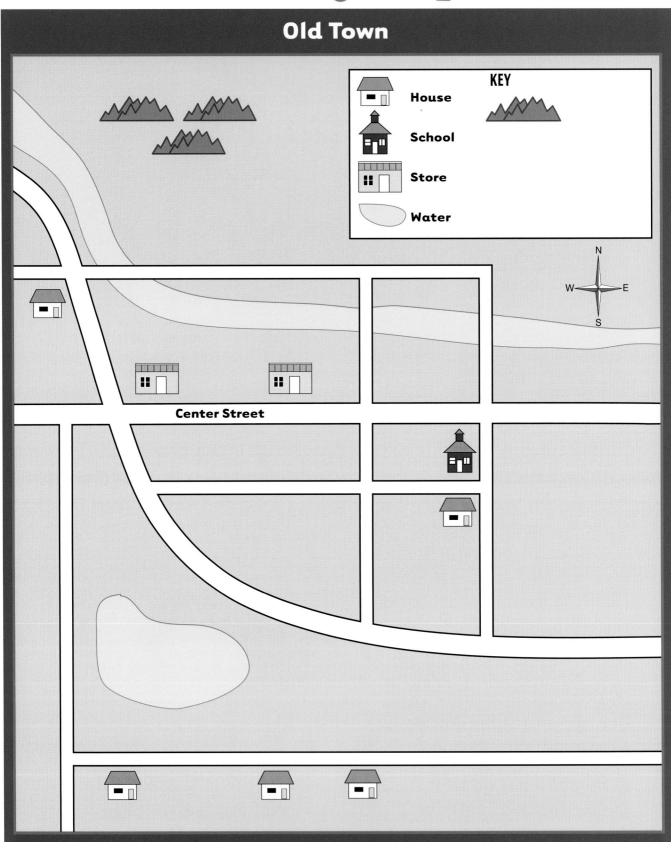

Jamie is writing a story about a made-up place called Old Town. She is making a map of the town. Can you help her?

 Map It!

Complete this map for Jamie.

1. What is missing on the compass rose? Add S, E, and W in the right places.

2. There is one school on the map. Old Town needs another school. Add a new school north of the old one.

3. Jamie wants a park in Old Town. Make a symbol for a park. Add it to the map key and show the park on the map. Is the park east or west of the new school? _____

4. Old Town needs a hospital. Add a symbol for a hospital to the map key and show it on the map. Is the hospital north or south of the old school? _____

5. The color blue is used for water on this map. How many bodies of water do you see in Old Town? _____ Give them names. (Remember the difference between a river and a lake!)

6. Old Town needs a fire station. Add a symbol for a fire station to the map key and show it on the map.

7. What does this stand for on the map? Add the word next to the symbol in the key. Put the word on the map, too.

8. Where would you like to live in Old Town? Add a new neighborhood. Show the houses and label your house.

9. Now draw the route from your house to your school. (You can decide whether you go to the old school or the new school.)

10. What else would you like to add to Old Town? Think of two more things or places to add. Make symbols for them and add them to the key and the map.

Think It Over

People who plan towns use maps. Why do you think maps help them?

What Is a Map Grid?

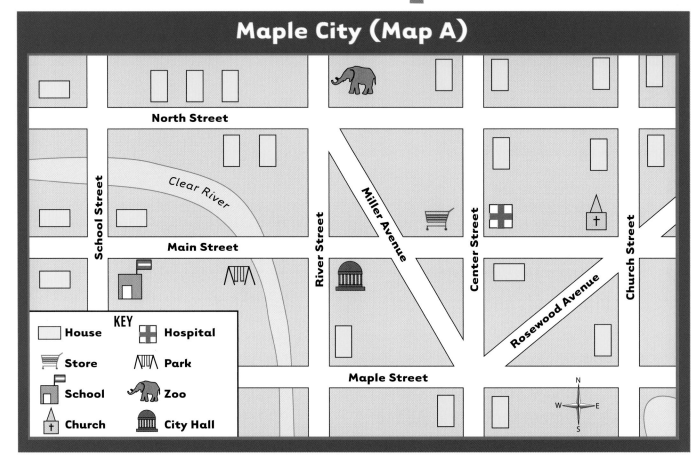

Maple City (Map A)

Here are two maps of Maple City. What is the difference between them? If you said that Map B has a pattern of squares on it, you are correct. The pattern of squares on Map B is called a **map grid**. A map grid helps you locate places.

First, let's find things without using a grid. Use Map A to locate these places.

Use Your Skills

1. The school is on the corner of Main Street and School Street. Circle it on the map.

2. Find City Hall on the map. Draw a ★ on the building.

3. The zoo is north of a store. Find the zoo on the map and write a ✓ by it.

Think It Over

What did you have to do in order to find places on Map A? What skills did you use?

Using a Grid

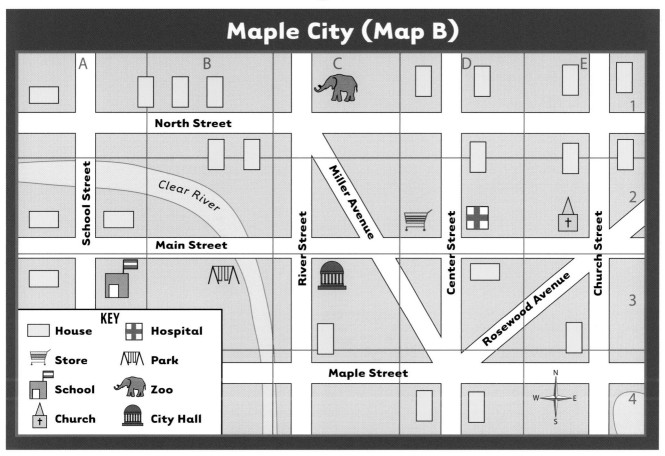

Maple City (Map B)

KEY
- ☐ House
- 🛒 Store
- 🏫 School
- ✝ Church
- ➕ Hospital
- 🛝 Park
- 🐘 Zoo
- 🏛 City Hall

Map B shows the same place that Map A does, but it also has a map grid. Lines running up and down and across the map create a pattern of squares. Each square has a letter and a number.

Let's use the grid to find the zoo. Find the letter **C** on the top of the grid. Find the number **1** along the side. Put your finger on the **C** and move it down until you are even with the **1**. The zoo is in box **C 1**.

 ## Use Your Skills

Find something that is in each box.

1. E 2 _____

2. C 3 _____

3. D 4 _____

 ## Think It Over

How can a grid help you read a map? Why might it be easier to find places on a city map with a grid?

Take a Walk in the City

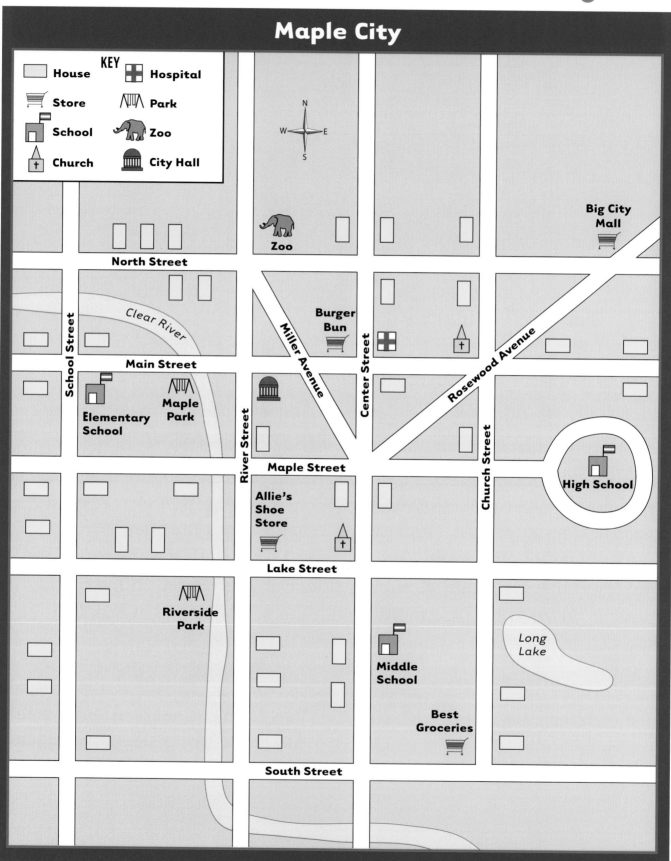

Maple City

KEY
- House
- Store
- School
- Church
- Hospital
- Park
- Zoo
- City Hall

Zoo

Big City Mall

North Street

School Street

Clear River

Main Street

Miller Avenue

Burger Bun

Center Street

Rosewood Avenue

River Street

Elementary School

Maple Park

Maple Street

Allie's Shoe Store

Church Street

High School

Lake Street

Riverside Park

Middle School

Long Lake

Best Groceries

South Street

Here is another map of Maple City. This map shows much more of the city. The labels are smaller, which means that it may be harder to read. A grid would really help on this map.

Jamie and Jordan sold cookies for their Scout troops. Now they have to deliver them. You can help.

 ## Map It!

Make a grid on this map of Maple City. Use a ruler to help you do it. For this grid, put the numbers on the top or bottom. Put the letters on one side.

Using the grid that you made, fill in the grid location for each place.

1. City Hall _____
2. Hospital _____
3. Elementary School _____

4. Middle School _____
5. High School _____
6. Big City Mall _____
7. Allie's Shoe Store _____
8. Best Groceries _____
9. Burger Bun _____
10. Zoo _____
11. Long Lake _____
12. Maple Park _____

 ## Think It Over

Does it matter whether the letters are on the top and bottom or on the left and right? Why or why not?

 ## Your Turn Now

Find a map of your town or state that does not have a grid. Photocopy part of the map and add a grid. Trade maps with a classmate. Ask each other questions using the grid.

What Is a Map Scale?

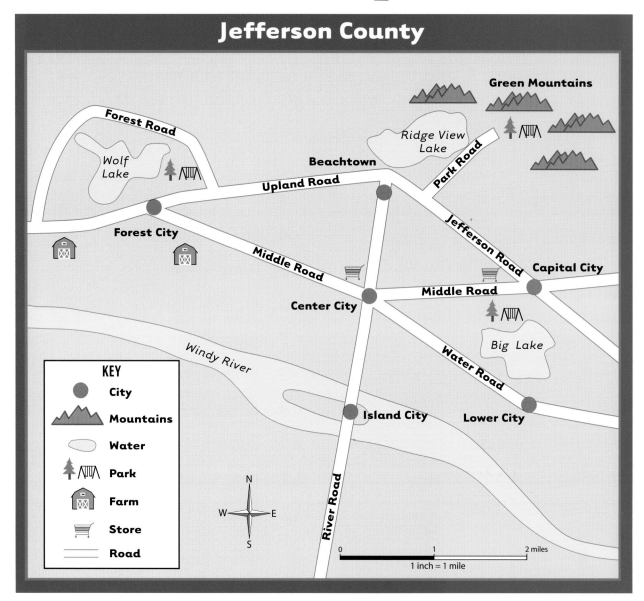

Jefferson County

We use maps to figure out **distance**. How far is it from here to there? Just by looking at a map, you can tell whether someplace is near or far. Look at the map above. You can see that Beachtown is near Ridge View Lake. You can see that the Green Mountains are far from Island City.

What if you want to know exactly how far apart two places are? Then you would need to use a map scale. A **map scale** helps you figure out exact distance.

This is a map scale.

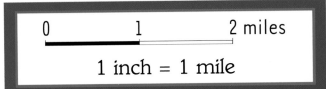

0   1   2 miles

1 inch = 1 mile

It says that 1 inch on this map equals 1 mile on Earth. If two places are 1 inch apart on the map, then they are 1 mile apart on Earth. On the map of Jefferson County, Beachtown is 1 inch away from Center City. This means that on Earth, the two places are 1 mile apart.

What if two places are 2 inches apart on the map? You can figure that out pretty quickly! On the map of Jefferson County, Center City is 2 inches from Lower City. So, Center City and Lower City are 2 miles apart on land.

Each map has its own scale. On this map 1 inch equals 1 mile. On another map, 1 inch might equal 10 miles or 200 miles.

Use Your Skills

You can use the map scale on this map to figure out distances in Jefferson County. Use a ruler to measure distances. Or, take the edge of a piece of paper and mark off 1 inch.

1. Measure the distance between Island City and Center City. How many inches is it? _____
So, how many miles apart are Island City and Center City?

_____

2. How many inches apart are Beachtown and Capital City? How many miles apart are they?

_____

3. How many inches apart are Forest City and Center City? How many miles apart are they?

_____

Think It Over

1. Why do different maps have different scales? Why aren't all map scales the same?

2. How would you find the distance to drive from Island City to Lower City? (Hint: Remember to stay on the roads!)

How Near, How Far?

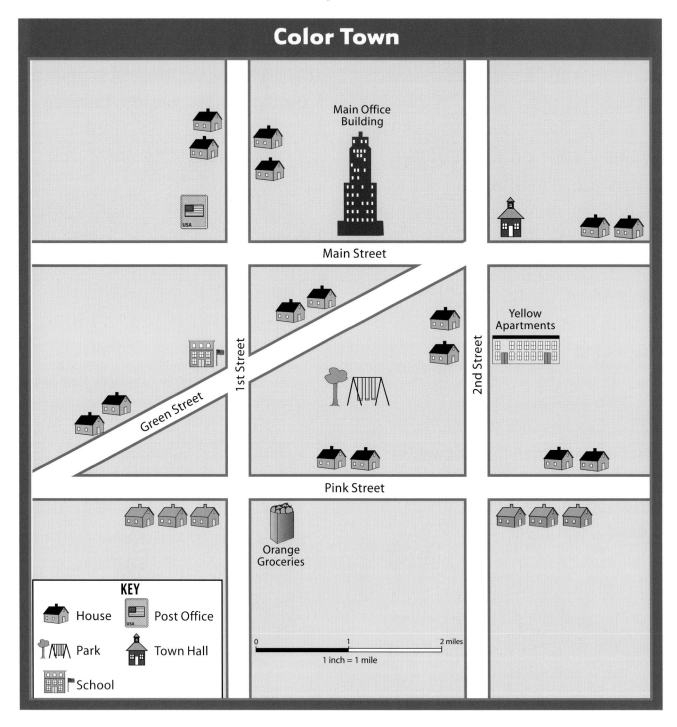

Color Town

This map shows you Color Town. Help the express mail driver figure out how far apart his deliveries will be.

Use Your Skills

Use the map of Color Town to answer these questions.

1. How far apart are Orange Groceries and the red houses on the map? _____

   How far apart are they on land?

   _____

2. The driver starts at the post office and drives to Town Hall. Measure the distance on the map. How far is it on land?

   _____

3. His next stop is Yellow Apartments. How far does he drive from Town Hall to Yellow Apartments? _____

4. If a bird flew from the school to the red houses, it wouldn't have to take the roads! Draw a straight line from the school to the red houses as a bird would fly. How far is that?

   _____

 **Map It!**

The driver wants to set up some new mailboxes. Add them to the map.

1. Draw a symbol for a mailbox and add it to the key.

2. Put one new mailbox 2 miles from the office building.

3. Put another new mailbox 3 miles from the blue houses.

4. How many miles does 1 inch represent on this scale? _____

```
0              10           20 miles
■■■■■■■■■■□□□□□□□□□□□□

      Map Scale
   1 inch = 10 miles
```

5. How many inches would a map with this scale need to show 300 miles? _____

```
0              300          600 miles
■■■■■■■■■■□□□□□□□□□□□□

      Map Scale
   1 inch = 300 miles
```

What Is a Political Map?

United States

This is a map of the United States. Because it shows states and countries, it is called a **political map**.

Look at the key and find the symbol for national border. A **border** divides one place from another. A national border is the boundary line between countries. Find Canada. It is north of the United States. Mexico is south of the United States.

Sometimes a border is an imaginary line. Sometimes a body of water forms part of a border. The Rio Grande forms part of the border between Mexico and the United States. The Atlantic Ocean and the Pacific Ocean are borders, too.

This map shows our 50 states. In the key, find the symbol for a state border. A state border separates one state from another.

Like national borders, state borders can be imaginary lines on a map. Bodies of water also separate states. Find the Mississippi River in the center of the United States. Follow the river from Minnesota to Louisiana to see how many states it separates. (The answer is ten!)

 ## Use Your Skills

Fill in the blanks with the correct word or symbol.

1. Canada is _____ of the United States.

2. Canada is _____ of Mexico.

3. The Atlantic Ocean is _____ of the United States.

4. The Pacific Ocean is on the _____ coast of the United States.

5. On this map the symbol for a national border is a line like this: _____ .

6. The _____ Ocean forms part of the border of Oregon.

7. The _____ Ocean forms part of the border of South Carolina.

8. Arizona shares a border with the state of _____ .

9. The Rio Grande forms the whole border between the state of _____ and the country of Mexico.

 ## Think It Over

Look at the border between Canada and the United States. Find the five large lakes near the border. These are the Great Lakes. The border runs through the middle of these lakes. What does that mean?

 ## Your Turn Now

Mapmakers use different symbols for borders. Find a map that uses other kinds of lines for state or national borders. Share it with the class.

Where Is Your State?

United States

There are 50 states in the United States. What is the name of your state? Write it here.

_____

My State

Where Are Alaska and Hawaii?

Alaska and Hawaii are two of the 50 states. Find them in the upper and lower left corners of the map of the United States. What are they doing there?

On the small map you can see that Alaska and Hawaii are separate from the other 48 states. Canada lies between Alaska and the "lower 48." Hawaii is a group of islands in the Pacific Ocean, far west of the other states.

It is hard to show all 50 states together on a small map. So mapmakers put Alaska and Hawaii in **inset maps** like these.

 ## Use Your Skills

Use the map on page 38 for these questions and activities.

1. Find your state on this map and circle its name.

2. Use a crayon or colored pencil to trace the borders all around your state.

3. Find Missouri on the map. Is Missouri north or south of Louisiana? _____

4. Is Louisiana east or west of Texas? _____

5. Which state is farthest north?

   _____

6. Which two of the lower 48 states are farthest south? _____

7. Does New York share a border with Canada or Mexico? _____

8. What ocean borders Hawaii? (Hint: Look at the inset map.)

   _____

There is only one city on this map. It is Washington, D.C. Washington is the capital of the United States. A capital is the city where government leaders meet.

What Is a Landform Map?

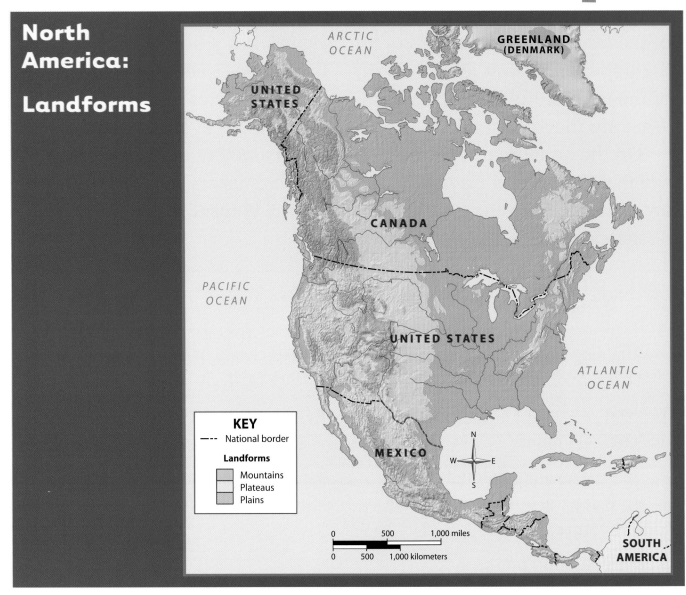

North America:

Landforms

ARCTIC OCEAN

GREENLAND (DENMARK)

UNITED STATES

CANADA

PACIFIC OCEAN

UNITED STATES

ATLANTIC OCEAN

MEXICO

KEY
- - - National border

Landforms
- Mountains
- Plateaus
- Plains

N
W   E
S

0   500   1,000 miles
0   500   1,000 kilometers

SOUTH AMERICA

This map of North America shows the landforms on our continent. **Landforms** are the shape of the land.

Look at the map key and find the symbol for mountains. It looks like this:

A large area or group of mountains is called a **mountain range**. One long mountain range stretches from Alaska almost down into South America. Put your finger on the most northern part of the United States. Trace the mountains all the way down.

 *Plains* are flat land.

 *Plateaus* are flat, high land.

 *Mountains* are the highest land.

 *Valleys* are areas of low land between hills or mountains.

 *Hills* are land that is higher than the land around them.

 *Islands* are land with water all around them.

The land along most of the coasts is flat. These are plains. The center of the United States is covered with plains, too.

Here are four new direction words:

northern—Jamie is in the northern part of the park.

southern—Jordan walked by the southern ball field.

western—The western side of the house is lighter.

eastern—The eastern corner is closer.

You can use them when you talk about landforms in North America.

Use Your Skills

Use the landform map to answer these questions.

1. Most of the mountains are in the _____ part of North America.

2. The Atlantic Ocean touches the _____ side of the United States.

3. Mexico is in the _____ part of North America.

4. Many islands are found in the _____ part of Canada.

5. The Arctic Ocean touches the _____ part of Canada.

Go Climb a Mountain!

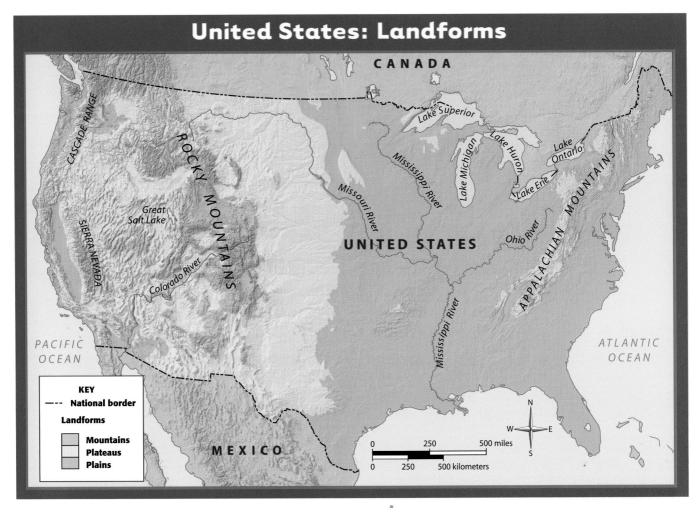

United States: Landforms

CANADA

CASCADE RANGE

ROCKY MOUNTAINS

SIERRA NEVADA

Great Salt Lake

Colorado River

Missouri River

Mississippi River

Lake Superior

Lake Michigan

Lake Huron

Lake Erie

Lake Ontario

UNITED STATES

Ohio River

APPALACHIAN MOUNTAINS

Mississippi River

PACIFIC OCEAN

ATLANTIC OCEAN

MEXICO

KEY
- - - **National border**

Landforms
- Mountains
- Plateaus
- Plains

0   250   500 miles
0   250   500 kilometers

N W E S

This is a landform map of the United States. You can see the landforms more closely on this map than on the map of North America.

The key on this map tells you what landforms the map shows. Find the symbol for plains in the key. Find plains areas on the map. Find the symbol for plateaus in the key. Find plateaus on the map.

Use Your Skills

1. Are the Appalachian Mountains east or west of the Rocky Mountains? _____

2. Where are there more mountains—in the eastern or the western part of the United States? _____

3. Find the Mississippi River. Does it run through plains or mountains?

_____

Title
_____

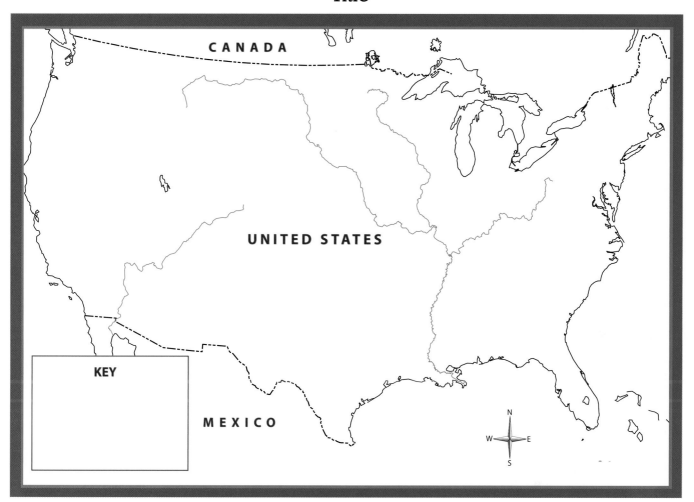

CANADA

UNITED STATES

KEY

MEXICO

 **Map It!**

You can make a landform map using this blank map.

1. Make a symbol for mountains and add it to the key.

2. Draw the western mountains on your map. Label them.

3. Now draw the eastern mountains and label them.

4. Make a symbol for plains and add it to the key. Color in the plains areas in the United States.

5. Make a symbol for plateaus and add it to the key. Color in the plateau areas in the United States.

6. Give your map a title.

Think It Over

Why does the map of the United States on page 42 have more detail than the map on page 40?

Review

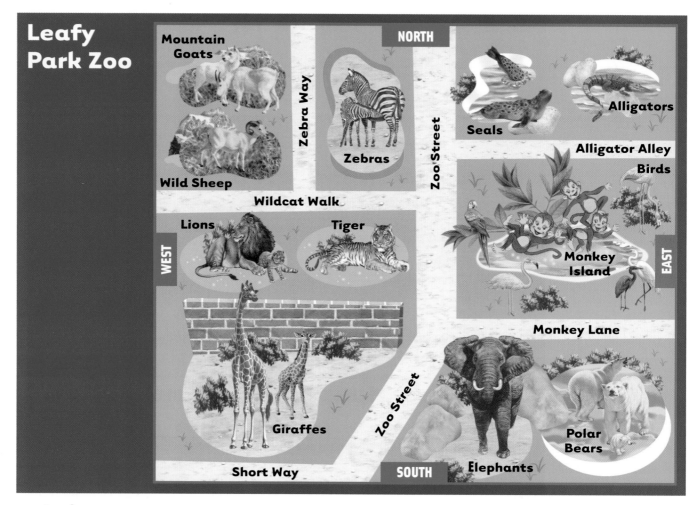

Leafy Park Zoo

Mountain Goats

Zebra Way

Wild Sheep

Wildcat Walk

Zebras

NORTH

Zoo Street

Seals

Alligators

Alligator Alley

Birds

WEST

Lions

Tiger

Monkey Island

EAST

Monkey Lane

Giraffes

Zoo Street

Short Way

SOUTH

Elephants

Polar Bears

 Map It!

Look at the picture map of Leafy Park Zoo on this page. It shows where you can find many different kinds of animals. The map on page 45 also shows Leafy Park Zoo, but some things are missing. It's your job to finish the map!

1. Fill in the correct directions at each side of the map.

2. Draw symbols to show where to find each kind of animal in the zoo. The animals should be in the same places as on the picture map.

3. Then draw your symbols in the key. Write what each symbol stands for.

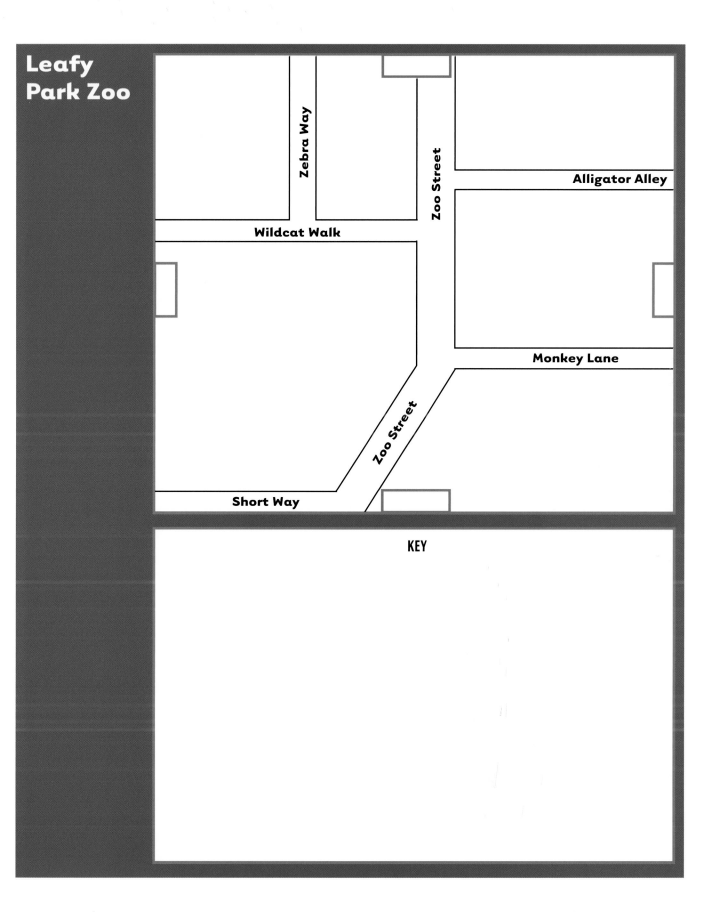

Leafy Park Zoo

Zebra Way

Zoo Street

Alligator Alley

Wildcat Walk

Monkey Lane

Zoo Street

Short Way

KEY

Review

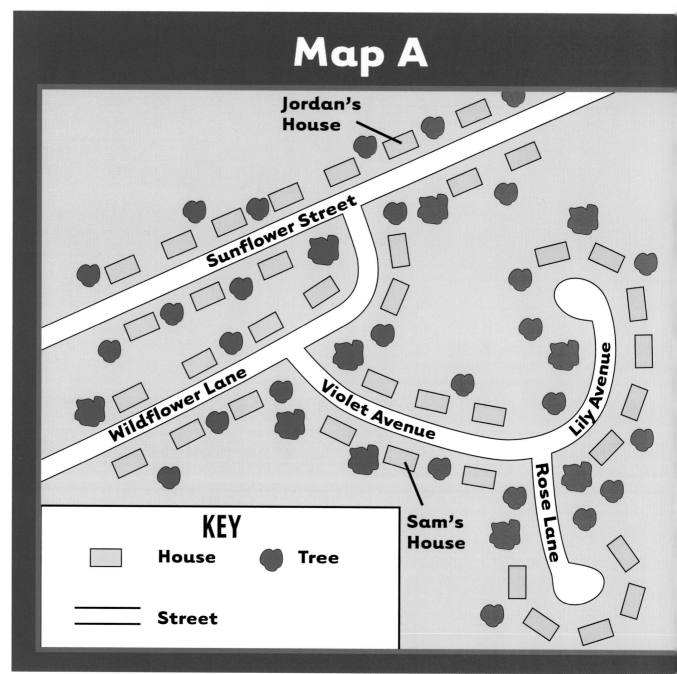

Map A

Jordan's House

Sunflower Street

Wildflower Lane

Violet Avenue

Lily Avenue

Rose Lane

Sam's House

KEY

House   Tree

Street

Comparing Maps

Look at Map A and Map B. Each statement is correct for one map. Circle the correct answer.

1. This map shows mountains.

Map A   Map B

2. This map uses the symbol for houses.

Map A   Map B

3. This map has a scale of one inch equals two miles.

Map A   Map B

Comparing Maps

Map B

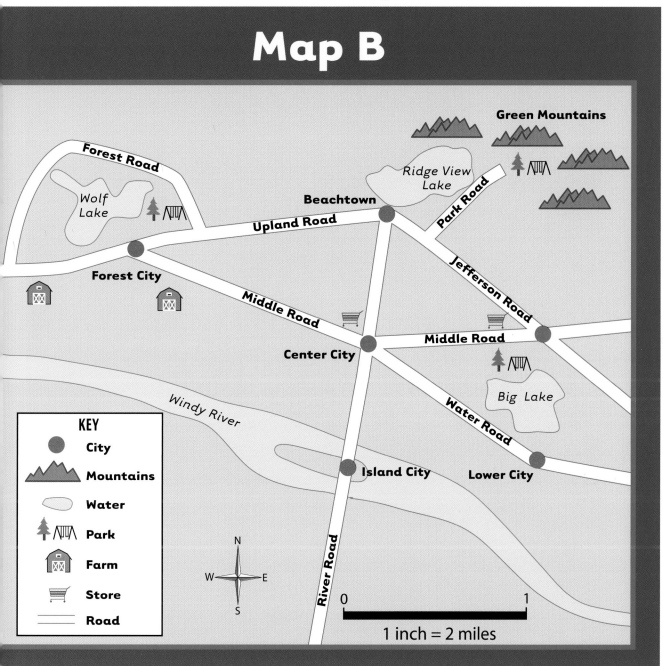

KEY
- ● City
- ⛰ Mountains
- 🟦 Water
- 🌲 Park
- 🏠 Farm
- 🛒 Store
- ── Road

1 inch = 2 miles

4. This map has a compass rose.

Map A   Map B

5. You could use this map to find your way to Jordan's house.

Map A   Map B

6. This map would be useful to plan your way between two cities.

Map A   Map B

7. This map shows lakes and a river.

Map A   Map B

Notes